# NORTH WALES FROM THE AIR

# NORTH WALES FROM THE AIR

WEBBAVIATION.CO.UK

breedon **books**
PUBLISHING

First published in Great Britain in 2008 by

The Breedon Books Publishing Company Limited

Breedon House, 3 The Parker Centre,

Derby, DE21 4SZ.

ISBN 978-1-85983-624-8

Printed and bound in Europe

## Acknowledgments

There are a number of people who have helped in the making of this book and I would like to express particular thanks to John Seville, the UK's best aerial photographic pilot, whose skill at flying 'photobatics' is legendary. I would also like to thank fellow aerial photographers William Cross and Catherine Wheildon for their constant support and my long-suffering partner Birgit Engsfeld for putting up with a world where only aerial photography is important!

# Contents

# Introduction

North Wales has always been a special place for me, having grown up with family holidays on the Lleyn Peninsula. In my mind's eye the sun always shone and the golden sands of Abersoch went on forever. As well as the sheer beauty of the place, North Wales has a wealth of history, much of it remarkably preserved, such as the Iron Age hut circles at Garn Boduan and the Roman forts like Canovium at Caerhun. Best known of all are the spectacular Norman castles at Conwy, Caernarfon, Beaumaris and Harlech. The images for the book were taken on several flights from 2006 onwards with a large number being specially taken on a very memorable flight in 2007. The flight was begun with some trepidation as our aerodrome at Barton, Manchester, was shrouded in thick mist, cloud and rain. The weather satellite showed sun in the west so I took one of my more reckless decisions and set off. We crossed the Welsh mountains in thick cloud and then suddenly broke out into fantastic clear sky with the most breathtaking scenery before us. It was distinctly more beautiful than Barnsley in cloud the day before! I then proceeded to empty the aircraft of fuel, my pockets of Compact flash cards and my bank balance of everything! The fruits of my labours you see here and I hope you enjoy looking at them as much as I enjoyed taking them.

**Previous page:** The town of Harlech with the castle perched on its cliff top.

**This page and left:** Harlech Castle. The town of Harlech is dominated by its castle, which was built between 1283 and 1289 by Edward I as part of his 'Iron Ring' of castles around Snowdonia. Designed by Master James of St George, the castle was defended by two concentric rings of inner and outer defences. Although now some distance from the coast, when it was originally constructed the sea came up to the foot of the cliffs, allowing the castle, like most of Edward's, to be supplied by ships during sieges. This allowed the castle to hold out during the Welsh uprising of 1294, when it was besieged by Madog ab Llewelyn's forces.

In 1404 the castle was captured by Owain Glyn Dŵr following a long siege, which left just 21 men alive in the castle when they eventually surrendered. He held the castle for four years, holding a parliament here until it was retaken by Henry of Monmouth in 1409, the future King Henry V.

The song *Men of Harlech* was inspired by the seven-year siege of the castle in 1468 during the Wars of the Roses, when the castle was held by the Lancastrians until their final surrender to the Yorkists. Harlech was the last Lancastrian castle to fall, and the siege was Britain's longest ever recorded.

Harlech was also the last castle to hold out for the Royalists during the English Civil War, finally surrendering in 1647. The victorious Parliamentarians ordered the demolition of the castle, but fortunately this was never carried out and it is now a protected World Heritage Site.

Portmeirion

Designed by Welsh architect Clough Williams-Ellis, Portmeirion was built between 1925 and 1973 using a mixture of architectural styles, although the overall effect is Italianate. The village is owned to this day by Williams-Ellis's descendants. The site was originally a foundry and boatyard which was converted into the modern village with additional buildings and the incorporation a number of salvaged architectural relics from other locations. The village is also noted for its surrounding woodland and gardens, which benefit from a mild climate that allows numerous exotic species to grow here.

Portmeirion has featured in numerous films and TV shows, most famously the cult 1960's series *The Prisoner,* which still draws many visitors to view the original shooting locations.

Porthmadog

**Above:** The Glaslyn Estuary, with Porthmadog on the left of the photograph.

Porthmadog, which translates to 'Maddocks' Port' in English, takes its name from its founder, William Maddocks, who reclaimed the land from the Glaslyn Estuary to build Tremadog and Porthmadog. The port was built between 1821 and 1825 and accounted for the town's prosperity, as it was used for shipping slate from Blaenau Ffestiniog to ports all over the world. To get the slate to the port a narrow gauge railway was built, the famous Ffestiniog Railway, which runs across 'The Cob', the great embankment that runs across the Glaslyn Estuary and took four years to build.

**Left:** Jet skis near Porthmadog.

Begun in 1832, the Festiniog Railway was quite an achievement. Difficult terrain forcing technical advances to be developed in the little railway, which were to influence many other railways. The 23.5in gauge was chosen to allow the wagons to negotiate the sharp curves as the track threads its way up the mountainside. Originally the wagons were horse drawn, but steam engines were introduced in 1863. The Ffestiniog line at first flourished but the eventual decline of the slate industry forced its closure in 1946. Fortunately it was saved by enthusiasts and reopened in 1954 to serve the tourist industry. The railway is now thriving, taking tourists into the breathtaking scenery of the Snowdonia National Park.

# Lleyn Peninsula

The first historical record of Criccieth was when Llewelyn Fawr built the first castle in the 13th century. It was taken by Edward I at the end of the century and the defences strengthened. It was held by the English until retaken by Owain Glyn Dŵr in 1403. The remains of the castle were retaken following the failure of the rebellion and remained in Crown hands until 1858 when they were sold. It is now preserved and maintained by CADW.

The area prospered in the 19th century as a result of shipping and the slate exports from nearby Porthmadog, with many of the crews and shipowners coming from the Criccieth area. The area grew further when the Cambrian Coast Railway arrived in 1867 and began the move towards tourism that is the mainstay of the town's economy today.

Tremadog Bay and the former Butlins Pwllheli. The holiday camp began life, during World War Two, as Admiralty training station HMS *Glendower*. The camp was built along the railway track and has its own station named Penychain. Many thousands of service men were stationed here, including HRH The Duke of Edinburgh, who later revisited the camp with the Queen in 1973.

The site became one of Billy Butlin's holiday camps after the war, opening in Easter 1947 with places for 5,000 holidaymakers. The camp soon grew, with capacity for up to 8,000, and included features such as a miniature railway to take guests to the beach, opened in 1953, and a chairlift, added in 1960.

In 1973 events took a more dramatic turn when there was a bad fire at the camp. Fortunately, this was extinguished by the fire brigade without any serious injuries and the camp soon bounced back. There was further drama in 1989 when the camp was hit by a tornado, causing two million pounds' worth of damage.

In the early 1990s, after a multimillion pound makeover, the camp was renamed Starcoast World and new features were added, including the large subtropical waterworld. The site continues to be a major asset to the local tourist industry, and in the late 1990s it was taken over by Haven Holidays and again remodelled and updated. It is now known as Hafan y Môr.

Further up the coast, to the left of the image, is Criccieth and on the far side of the bay, opposite the holiday camp, lies Harlech.

Pwllheli is the largest town on the Lleyn Peninsula and has been the location of an important market going back centuries. The town gained its Borough Charter from the Black Prince in 1355. By the 19th century the town was an important fishing port and ship-building centre, with a lifeboat station being established in 1891. The tourist industry started at the end of the century with the arrival of the Cambrian Coast Railway and tourism is today the mainstay of the town's economy. The promenade was developed during this period and there was even a tramway linking Pwllheli to Llanbedrog, which ran until it was destroyed by a storm in 1927. In 1925 Plaid Cymru, the Party of Wales, was founded here.

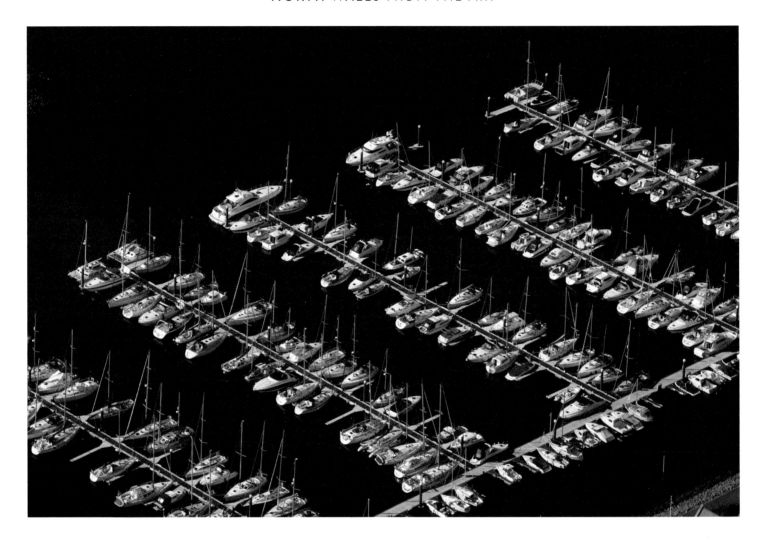

The biggest development the town has seen in recent years is the new Hafen Pwllheli, constructed in the early 1990s, which has deep-water berths in its marina for over 400 yachts. The area provides some of the best sailing waters in the UK with the undeveloped coastline designated as an area of outstanding natural beauty. The waters have played host to the British, European and World sailing championships and the Hafen has been awarded both Blue Flag status and the five Gold Anchors. The Hafen contains an active sailing club, numerous chandlery shops and every conceivable boatyard facility for yachtsmen.

**Left:** Best known for its beaches, Abersoch is a popular tourist destination for beach holidays and water sports, particularly sailing, windsurfing and jet skiing. The area is often referred to as the 'Welsh Riviera' or occasionally as 'Wilmslow-on-Sea' owing to its popularity with the Cheshire set.

Originally a fishing port, tourism became the mainstay of the economy in the 20th century, and Abersoch's popularity peaked in the 1970s, when the beaches were crammed full of sunbathers who flooded in from English cities. Numbers have fallen since the advent of low-cost foreign package holidays, but Abersoch and much of the rest of North Wales have found new ways to attract tourists, such as offering water sports and short breaks. Out of the tourist season, Abersoch hosts numerous cultural and educational events, including the Abersoch Jazz Festival.

Abersoch has three beaches, and the main beach at Morfa Gors is popular because of its easterly views of the St Tudwals Islands. The beach huts are highly sought after: despite having no water or electricity, a strip of beach with planning permission for a hut was recently sold for £63,000.

**Overleaf:** Abersoch's warren beach is the largest of the three. The smallest, harbour beach, is situated below it on the mouth of the River Soch, a busy spot for boat launchings.

**Above:** One of many quiet beaches around Abersoch.

**Left:** The old lifeboat at Penrhyn Du station, built in 1894 at a cost of £1,350. The watch room was added in 1897 and the station was closed in 1931. It has now been converted to a house. The palm trees and Monkey Puzzle tree show the warm climate of the area. A new lifeboat station was established in Abersoch in 1965, with a new boathouse being built in 1978 and a further new one being built in 1994. To this day the RNLI keeps watch over the seas around Abersoch.

Just off shore from Abersoch lie the two islands of St Tudwals. They have been occupied since Roman times and house the remains of a monastery. The islands are named after a sixth-century resident, St Tudwal. In the days of sail, the area saw a large number of shipwrecks and so, in 1877, a lighthouse was erected on St Tudwals West. This was manned up until 1935. In 1922 a 'sun valve' was installed, which turned the light off during daylight. Today the lighthouse runs off solar power. Occasionally dolphins and porpoises can be seen in the waters off the islands. Although significant numbers of these animals remain in Cardigan Bay, the species is in decline in Europe as a whole, largely due to pollution and being caught in fishing nets.

**Above:** On the north side of the Lleyn Peninsula lie the spectacular remains of the Iron Age hillfort of Garn Boduan. The fort is built on a volcanic hill with a perimeter wall defence, within which lie the remains of more than 100 stone structures, predominantly rings of stone that formed the basis of Iron Age round houses. There is evidence of occupation from the Iron Age and into the Roman period and it is probable that, as the Romans were not especially active on the Lleyn Peninsula, they allowed the local population to defend themselves against seaborne raiders.

**Overleaf:** The hillfort is adjacent to the village of Nefyn, which used to be a very active fishing port, catching and salting herring for eager markets in Liverpool and the rest of England.

# Anglesey

**Above:** Holy Island with Trearddur Bay centre right and Holyhead Mountain in the background. The island is so named because of the high number of ancient religious sites, including standing stones and burial chambers. The area is also an important wildlife habitat, particularly the rocky cliffs and coastal cliff heathland, which are home to a number of rare species such as the spotted rock-rose, *Tuberaria guttata*.

**Previous page:** Holyhead Mountain and South Stack Lighthouse. At 720 feet high, Holyhead mountain is the highest point on Anglesey and on a clear day you can see the Isle of Man from here. The lighthouse was built in 1809 at a cost of £12,000. Originally it was accessed by means of a rope and basket system, but eventually a bridge was built. In 1984 the lighthouse became remotely controlled from the Trinity House Operational Control Centre in Harwich, Essex.

Isallt Bach, Trearddur Bay, one of Anglesey's most popular coastlines. Trearddur Bay translates as 'Arthur's Bay' in English. Trearddur Bay and its adjacent coves are popular for sailing and scuba diving.

Holyhead is the gateway to Ireland, with a very busy ferry port that has a history of connecting Britain to Ireland going back 4,000 years. The Romans built a coastal fort here on which St Cybi later built a Christian monastery. The Roman walls are very well preserved and today surround St Cybis church, parts of which date back to the 13th century.

The seaward approaches to the port are dominated by the 2 ½ mile-long breakwater, built between 1845 and 1873, which makes Holyhead a welcome refuge in a storm. The breakwater was then the largest in Europe, cost 20 workers lives and involved moving 7 million tons of stone from Holyhead Mountain and Moelfre. The construction was visited by Queen Victoria in 1865 and the liner *Great Eastern* in 1859.

**Above:** The £6.2m Celtic Gateway Project is the newest addition to the port, with the construction of a harbour causeway and the Celtic Gateway Bridge to link the ferry terminal and station to the town centre. The bridge is a landmark structure made from stainless steel and imported from Italy. The station is the western terminus of the North Wales Coast line, built in 1851 and now linked directly with the High Street, in close proximity to St Cybis Church and the Roman fort, which you can see in the top centre of the photograph.

**Right:** This photo of the Holyhead Hotspur football stadium was taken on Saturday 6 October 2007, during a match against Bala Town. Holyhead Hotspur won!

**Above:** Malltraeth with the River Cefni, which was canalised in 1824. The farmland was drained and 'Maltraeth Cob' Dyke was built in 1810. The area and its remaining marshland are now an important wildlife habitat and officially designated as a Site of Special Scientific Interest. The area has been inhabited since prehistoric times and a megalith stands adjacent to the railway line in the centre of the image.

**Left:** Rhoscolyn with its lifeboat station, which stands as a reminder of the five lifeboatmen who lost their lives on 3 December 1920, trying to rescue the crew of the steamship *Trimbo* in a severe storm.

**Above:** Dwyran with the Menai Strait behind.

**Left:** Plas Newydd was designed by James Wyatt in the 18th century, in a mixture of classical and Gothic styles. Home of the Marquesses of Anglesey, its most famous occupant, Henry William Paget (1768-1854) the 1st Marquess of Anglesey, commanded the cavalry at the Battle of Waterloo and was second in command to the Duke of Wellington. Relics of the battle are now contained in a museum here, including the blood-spattered trousers he wore when he lost a leg in the battle. The house also contains a collection of Rex Whistler paintings, including his largest, as the artist was a close friend of the 6th Marquess. The 7th Marquess gave the house and its extensive gardens to the National Trust in 1976 and it is now one of Anglesey's top tourist attractions.

Llanfairpwllgwyngyllgogerychwyrndrobwllllantysiliogogogoch is the longest place name in Great Britain and translates into English as 'Saint Mary's Church in the hollow of the white hazel near a rapid whirlpool and the Church of St Tysilio of the red cave'. The name was invented in the mid-19th century as a station name to attract tourists, a gimmick that has been a success. In the centre right of the image is the Marquess of Anglesey's Column, built to commemorate the 1st Marguess of Anglesey's exploits at Waterloo.

Originally constructed by Robert Stephenson in 1846 to 1850, the Britannia was a wrought-iron tubular bridge with rectangular box-section spans. These box sections were the largest in existence at the time. Unfortunately the tubes were protected from the elements by a wooden roof covered in tar. Surprisingly this highly combustible feature remained intact until 1970 when it was (probably) set on fire by two small boys on a nature expedition. The bridge was rebuilt and the tubes were replaced with a conventional girder arch. This was not possible in the original design, which had to be high enough for the large sailing vessels of the day. The new design allowed a road deck above the railway line, which now carries the main A55 road.

**Above:** Ynys Gored Goch and the Menai Strait, showing the strong tidal currents. The island is almost flooded during the high spring tide, with water coming right up to, and occasionally into, the house.

**Right:** The Menai Suspension Bridge, built in 1826 to a design by Thomas Telford, was the first fixed connection to the mainland. It was built to meet growing demand for the route to Ireland via Holyhead and to replace the dangerous ferry crossings that had caused the loss of many lives. The bridge was the first large-scale suspension bridge and one of the architectural wonders of its age. Originally built with a wooden road deck and iron chains, the road deck was replaced with steel in 1893 and the iron chains were replaced with steel ones in 1938.

**Above:** The RV *Prince Madog* docked in Menai Bridge. The ship is operated by the University of Wales and the VT Group. She is used for research in oceanographic biology, geology, chemistry and sea physics and carries up to 20 students and 10 scientists.

**Left:** The town of Menai Bridge pre-dates the bridge by many centuries. Known as Porthaethwy before the bridge was built and to this day in Welsh, the location is the shortest crossing point on the Menai Strait and it is therefore likely that there has been a settlement here since Roman times.

**Above:** The town of Beaumaris pre-dates the Norman castle and was originally a Viking settlement called 'Porth y Wygyr', which translates as 'Port of the Vikings' in English. The town is also noted for its Gaol Museum, on the left of the photograph, and next to it the 14th-century St Mary's Church.

**Previous page:** Beaumaris Castle was the last of Edward I's castles in North Wales and was never fully completed. Work stopped in 1298 before the towers and gatehouses had reached their full height. The castle was built to a very sophisticated concentric ring design with an inner and outer ward, surrounded by a moat and with a tidal dock which allowed the castle to be resupplied directly from the sea.

Beaumaris pier was built in 1846 to a design in wood and iron by Frederick Foster. During its heyday in the late 19th and early 20th centuries it was larger, with a landing stage for shipping at the end. The pier was kept busy with the steamships and passengers of the Liverpool and North Wales Steamship Company until that trade declined after World War Two. The landing stage was demolished in the 1960s. Today the pier has been restored and preserved by the local council.

Next to the pier is the Beaumaris lifeboat station, which was established in 1891 and currently operates an 'Atlantic 85' rigid inflatable lifeboat funded by viewers of the BBC children's television programme *Blue Peter*.

**Above:** Today, the town is enjoying developments of a more peaceful nature with new waterside developments along the Victoria Dock.

**Left:** The strategic importance of Caernarfon was recognised long before the Normans arrived. The Roman fort of Segontium was built in AD77 by General Agricola and in use until the end of the Roman occupation around AD400.

**Previous page:** Caernarfon is dominated by its 13th-century castle. The greatest of those built by Edward I, it bears a striking resemblance to Constantinople. In 1294, during the Welsh rebellion, the castle was taken and burned by Madog ap Llywelyn before it was even completed. It was retaken and finished by Edward in around 1330. Owain Glyn Dŵr laid siege to it in 1403 and 1404, but failed to take it. The Royalists were less successful during the Civil War, surrendering to the besieging Parliamentarians in 1646.

Today Caernarfon enjoys a peaceful existence and is adored by millions of visitors for its sleepy Welsh charm, which contrasts with the nearby big cities of Liverpool and Manchester. It was originally the site of a Celtic church inaround the fifth century. The original town was constructed, including its town wall, along with the building of the castle. The port prospered in the 19th century, shipping slate from the quarries nearby to destinations all over the world.

At the bottom right of the image is Caernarfon Station on the Welsh Highlands Railway. This is an ongoing project to reopen the railway, which closed in the 1930s, through to Porthmadog and link it to the Ffestiniog Railway. Already halfway to completion, the railway should be open all the way by 2009. Much work has to be done to open the station as the original Welsh Highland Railway had ended at Dinas Junction, three miles away. The new Caernarfon Station was built on the site of the former standard gauge railway and was opened in 1997.

In 1911 the local MP, David Lloyd George, came up with the idea of having Royal Investitures take place within Caernarfon. The first one took place on 13 July 1911 with the investiture of the future King Edward VIII, and the most recent was that of Prince Charles, current Price of Wales, on 1 July 1969.

At the lower centre of the image is the Caernarfon tunnel, built in 1854. Originally built as a railway tunnel for the Bangor and Caernarfon Railway, it was converted between 1994 and 1998 into a road tunnel to help reduce the number of cars travelling through the town centre.

**Above:** Bangor pier, opened in 1896, was one of the last to be completed in the UK and is now one of the best preserved.

**Left:** Bangor City Football Club playing against Llandyrnog United in October 2007.

**Previous page:** Bangor's history goes back to the founding of its cathedral in the sixth century and today is dominated by its university, which has almost as many students as there are townsfolk.

**Overleaf:** Despite its Norman looks Penrhyn Castle was actually built by Thomas Hopper in 1820–1845 for the Pennant family, although it does incorporate parts of much older buildings.

Conwy

Conwy is one of the most impressive mediaeval walled towns in Europe and a listed World Heritage site. The castle and town were built by Edward I on the site of the Aberconwy monastery, with the abbey church being turned into the parish church of St Mary's (above). The town contains a number of architectural gems, including the smallest house in Britain; Plas Mawr (centre of previous page with the white tower), one of the best preserved Elizabethan town houses; and of course the bridges. The first bridge was the suspension bridge built by Thomas Telford in 1826. This was followed in 1849 by Robert Stephenson's tubular railway bridge. During World War One a practice pontoon bridge was erected where the final modern road bridge was built in 1958.

**Above:** In more recent years Conwy has seen two major construction projects, the marina and the A55 tunnel which now allows through traffic to bypass the town and avoid the mass traffic crawl that used to prevail in the 1970s. The marina was opened in 1992 and has pontoon berths for 500 vessels. During World War Two the giant floating Mulberry harbours were built here on the Conwy Morfa and floated out into the River Conwy.

**Overleaf:** Further up the river at Caerhun lies the Roman fort of Canovium, built in around AD75 to protect the original crossing point of the river. It remained in use for the remainder of the Roman occupation. The 14th-century St Marys Church now stands in one corner of the fort, and above and to the right you can still see traces of the quay and harbour. In between lay quite an extensive vicus (settlement).

**Above and overleaf:** Llandudno is the largest of the Welsh seaside resorts, adored by visitors for its Victorian architecture, particularly the Grade II listed pier, built in 1878.

**Left:** Although a quite place today, Deganwy has had its share of interesting history. In the sixth century it was the capital of Gwynedd under Maelgwn Gwynedd, who had his stronghold on the castle hill in the upper left of the image. The castle was destroyed and rebuilt several times as it changed hands between the English and the Welsh. Edward I finally demolished the remains when he built Conwy Castle.

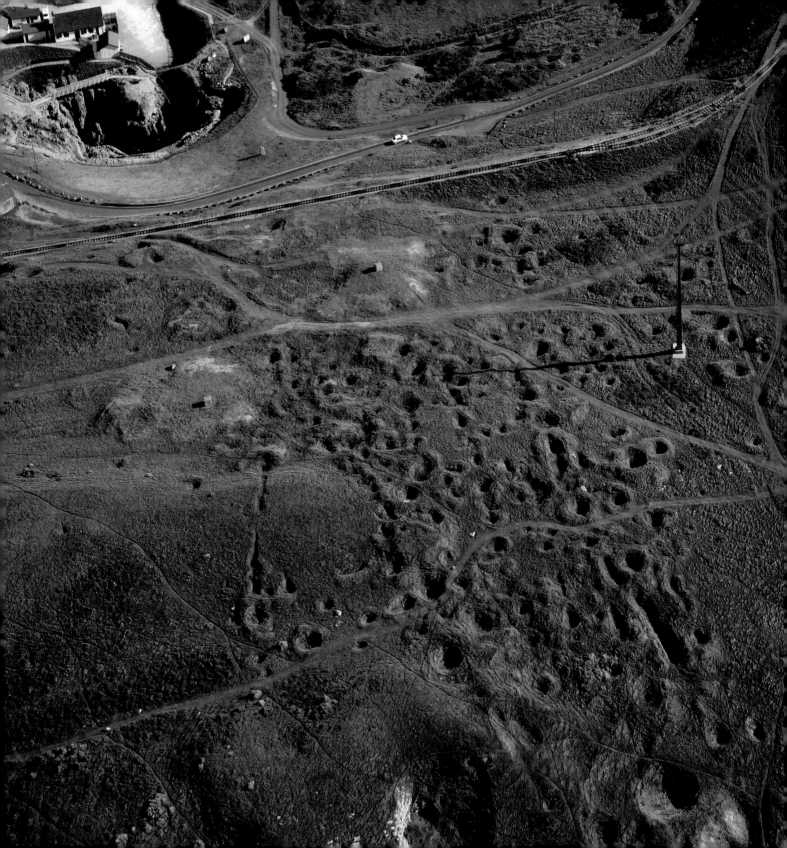

**Left:** At the far end of the Great Orme sits this cliff-top lighthouse, which was built in 1862 and was in use until 1985. The building is now a guest house.

**Opposite:** The Great Orme has been mined for centuries, and the limestone rock contains rich seams of copper ore. The surface is pock-marked with bell pit excavations. In the top left of the photograph is the prehistoric open-cast mine and the Bronze Age Mining Centre, with its entrance into the underground mine workings. It is the only Bronze Age mine in Europe open to the public.

Discovered in 1987 during landscaping work, these deeper mine shafts date back 4,000 years and are still being explored by archaeologists. With at least 16km of tunnels discovered so far, it is thought that they are the world's largest prehistoric mines and may have accounted for a significant proportion of the copper around during the Bronze Age. Bronze is an alloy of copper, made by heating Malachite, a green copper ore, and usually blending it with tin, so the Great Orme would have been a very important place at the time. Thousands of stone hammers and antler tools have been found, with much of the workings still showing hand-tool marks. The mines were probably worked throughout the Bronze Age (2100 to 700BC) and parts were mined in the 17th, 18th and 19th centuries. Spoil from the later workings had covered the site, but it has now been cleared away to reveal the original tunnel entrances.

**Above:** Colwyn Bay, looking along the northern Welsh coast towards Llandulas with Rhyl in the distance and the offshore windfarm in Liverpool bay on the horizon.

**Right:** St Michael's Church in Abergele. Rebuilt in 1878, it stands on the site of an ancient Celtic monastery. The churchyard contains a mass grave for the 33 victims of the Abergele train disaster, which occurred on 20 August 1868 when a runaway group of wagons carrying paraffin hit a passenger train, causing a fatal explosion and fire. At the time it was the country's worst rail disaster.

Pen-y-Corddyn-Mawr is the largest of a number of Iron Age hillforts guarding the northern borders of Wales. Located on the plateau of a limestone hill, the fort is surrounded almost entirely by cliffs, which form an excellent natural defence. With an area of 37 hectares, it might have housed more than 1,000 people. It was probably constructed around the first century BC, although there is some debate that it may be much older, perhaps from the late Bronze Age, around the ninth century BC. Much is uncertain about the fort, and the only significant archaeological excavation took place in 1906. The defences consisted of a double ring of ramparts, with the higher ramparts having a substantial wall with a fighting platform on top. The main entrance can be seen on the left, protected by in-turned ramparts that would have allowed a good field of fire against any attacker trying to storm the gate. Coins and other artifacts from the late Roman period have been found at the site, indicating Roman influence or occupation near the end of their occupation of Britainm in the late fourth and early fifth centuries. The adjacent hill at the bottom left of the image is Cefn yr Ogof, which has been extensively mined for lead. It is possible that this mining dates back to Roman times and could explain why there was so much Roman activity here. The hillfort is now partially surrounded by the village of Rhyd-y-foel, which can be seen on the lower right of the image.

The caravan parks at Towyn are among the largest in Wales. Towyn was badly affected by flooding in 1990, when part of the sea wall collapsed due to great pressure from the unusually high tide and strong gale force wind. The area has since been restored and flood defences improved.

The sea has other interesting tales to tell. Just off the coast at this point lie the remains of the *Resurgam II*, probably the oldest submarine still in existence. Built in 1878 with a displacement of 30 tons and steam driven, she was the first modern submarine and sank off the coast here on 25 February 1880, while under tow to Portsmouth for evaluation.

**Above, left and previous page:** Rhyl. Largely a tourist destination for holidaymakers and day trippers from nearby Liverpool, Rhyl has been a popular resort since Victorian times. Recent decades have been more economically challenging, with competition from package foreign holidays, and the town has received some major investments to help it compete in the modern tourist industry. A key development has been the Rhyl Events Arena, left, which opened in 1994 as part of a multimillion pound redevelopment. The arena is 80 meters wide and can hold up to 8,000 people. The maze is made from some 380,000 individual paving blocks.

The town of Rhuddlan (above) grew up on the crossing point of the River Clwyd and, because of this strategic location, it was here in 1277 that Edward built Rhuddlan Castle (left). Like most of Edward's castles, it was designed to be supplied by ships from the sea, although other aspects of the castle design are quite different from the others, particularly its distinctive concentric diamond shape with gatehouses in the corners rather than along the curtain wall. The castle replaced an earlier motte and bailey castle, which lies just to the right after the trees in the above image and many believe occupies the site of Gruffydd ap Llywelyn's palace. This earlier castle was built by Robert of Rhuddlan in 1073 to consolidate the Norman invasion.

**Above:** The Marble Church opened in 1860, is dedicated to St Margaret, and was built by Lady Willoughby de Broke in memory of her husband at a cost of £60,000. The outside of the church is actually limestone, with the church's name coming from the 13 varieties of marble used in the interior. The churchyard contains the remains of numerous soldiers from the nearby Kinmel Park camp. Some died in the 1918 Spanish flu pandemic and some were killed in a riot caused by poor conditions and bureaucratic delays in shipping Canadian troops home after World War One.

**Left and previous page:** Bodelwyddan Castle was built between 1830 and 1852 and is today an outpost of the National Portrait Gallery. During World War One it was used for troop training. The haunting remains of their practice trenches are a silent memorial to those who built them and never returned.

St Asaph, or Llanelwy in Welsh, developed from a monastery founded in the sixth century by Saint Kentigern. The original church was destroyed by Henry II in 1245, again by Edward I in 1282 and finally by Owain Glyn Dŵr in 1402. The current cathedral, Britain's smallest, was erected on the site in the 14th century and has some Victorian alterations. It was here that Bishop Morgan translated the Bible into Welsh in 1558. Although officially a town, St Asaph is seeking city status, which will make it one of the UK's smallest cities. The local economy has enjoyed some recent prosperity since the coming of the A55 dual carriageway, which means the town is now a quick journey from the big cities of England.

**Above:** The airstrip used by the Denbigh Gliding Club at Lleweni Parc.

**Left and previous page:** Moel-y-Gaer hillfort near Bodfari is one of a number of Iron Age hillforts that form part of a defensive chain along the summits of the Clwydian Hills. Running alongside Moel-y-Gaer is the Offa's Dyke path, which follows as closely as possible the defensive dyke built by King Offa of Mercia in the eighth century, which marked the boundary between the kingdom of Mercia and the kingdom of Powys.

**Overleaf:** Denbigh.

Most of what we see of Denbigh and its castle today dates from the time of Edward I, but it is probable that the castle was built on the site of an earlier Welsh castle. The name Denbigh comes from the Welsh 'Dinbych', or 'little fort' in English, so the site may have been fortified for quite some time before Edward arrived.

During the Wars of the Roses, Denbigh was initially held by Jasper Tudor, Earl of Pembroke, Henry VI's half-brother. He lost the town in 1460 but returned in 1468 with an army of 2,000 Welshmen and burned the town to the ground.

Originally the town lay entirely within the walls, but civilian buildings soon grew up outside and after the town's destruction the town centre moved downhill to its present location, centred around the market.

During the English Civil War the town was held by William Salisbury for the Royalists, with a force of local men. After the Royalist defeat at Rowton, Charles I took brief refuge in Denbigh Castle. After he left, the castle continued to hold out until it finally capitulated to the Parliamentarians in 1646, leaving the castle and town walls in ruins.

All that remains of St Hilary's Church is the tower, the rest having been demolished in 1923. Prior to demolition it was a fairly substantial building, although much modified over the years so that little of the original 14th-century garrison chapel remained. In 1874 St Mary's Church was built as a replacement and St Hilary's became dilapidated. The chapel was built on solid rock so was unusual in that no graveyard was possible. Funerals took place at anther church instead.

The remains of the western town wall, and within them Leicester's Church. In 1563 Elizabeth I made Robert Dudley, Earl of Leicester, Baron of Denbigh. His oppressive local rule led to some disturbances with the locals, which resulted in several being tried and beheaded. To calm the situation Elizabeth granted the inhabitants a charter of rights and the Earl, to make amends, began construction of a church in 1579. He had intended that the church should become a cathedral, taking over from that in St Asaph, but although some considerable work was done on the building it was never completed and remains an unfinished ruin to this day.

**Above:** Ruthin Gaol, built in 1775 to replace an earlier one from 1684, contained both a treadmill and a padded cell. At least one execution took place here when, on 17 Febuary 1903, William Huges, a local man, was executed for shooting dead his wife. The largest part of the gaol, the Pentonville-style wing, was added in 1866 with cells for 100 prisoners. One prisoner, John Jones, known as the Welsh Houdini, managed to escape from the prison twice. The gaol closed in 1916 and was used as a munitions factory during World War Two. It is now preserved and parts of it are open to the public.

**Previous page:** Ruthin looking north-east with the Clwydian Range behind.

**Right:** St Peter's Square, with its clock tower erected in 1885. Behind the tower is the 16th-century Myddleton Arms, with its distinctive Dutch-style dormer roof. To the right is the Georgian-style Castle Hotel.

St Peter's Church was established by John de Grey in the 14th century, with the oldest parts of the building dating back to 1310. The building was damaged in September 1400 when Owain Glyn Dŵr burnt Ruthin at the start of the Welsh rebellion. Much of what can presently be seen dates from the 18th and 19th centuries, particularly the rebuilding work done by R.K. Penson from 1854 to 1859. He built the belfry, spire, the south porch and the roofs.

Built in 1889–91 the Tabernacle Welsh Presbyterian Chapel is noted for its striking round architectural style, which is particularly evident from above. It is one of only two round or partially round chapels in Wales and the interior is noted for its large organ, hammer beam roof and semi-circular pews. When new it cost £1,841 and a number of houses had to be demolished to make way for it.

**Above:** Ruthin School is one of the UK's oldest public schools. The collegiate school was founded by Reginald de Grey, shortly after Edward I's conquest of Wales. The school survived the burning of the town by Owain Glyn Dŵr in 1400 and functioned until it was dissolved by Henry VIII in 1535. In 1574, in the reign of Elizabeth I, it was refounded by Gabriel Goodman, the Dean of Westminster. The school moved to the site in the photograph in the early 1890s.

**Left:** The town centre with Clwyd Street in the bottom left corner and St Peter's Square and Well Street running from the lower centre to the right of the image. The very large polygonal building in the middle of the image is the new Denbighshire County Council headquarters and the half-timbered building opposite and below right of the clock tower is the old courthouse, built in 1404 and previously the town's execution site.

**Overleaf:** Ruthin Castle. Begun by Dafydd ap Gruffydd in 1277, it was largely demolished following the Civil War.

**Above:** The Llangollen Railway depot is a treasure trove of railway history. Closed by Dr Beeching in 1964, the railway was reopened in 1981 and will soon reach as far as Corwen. In the top left of the image is the site of Llangollen's International Musical Eisteddfod.

**Left:** Valle Crucis Cistercian Abbey, established in 1201 and dissolved by Henry IV in 1537.

**Previous page:** The River Dee meandering through Llangollen. In the background is the Llangollen Canal and to the centre left is the station, which opened in 1865 and is now part of the preserved Llangollen railway.

**Overleaf:** Castell Dinas Bran was built by the princes of Powys in the late 13th century to replace an earlier structure. The castle stands on the site of an Iron Age hillfort. The castle had a very short life, being badly damaged in the war against Edward I, and was abandoned at the end of the 13th century.

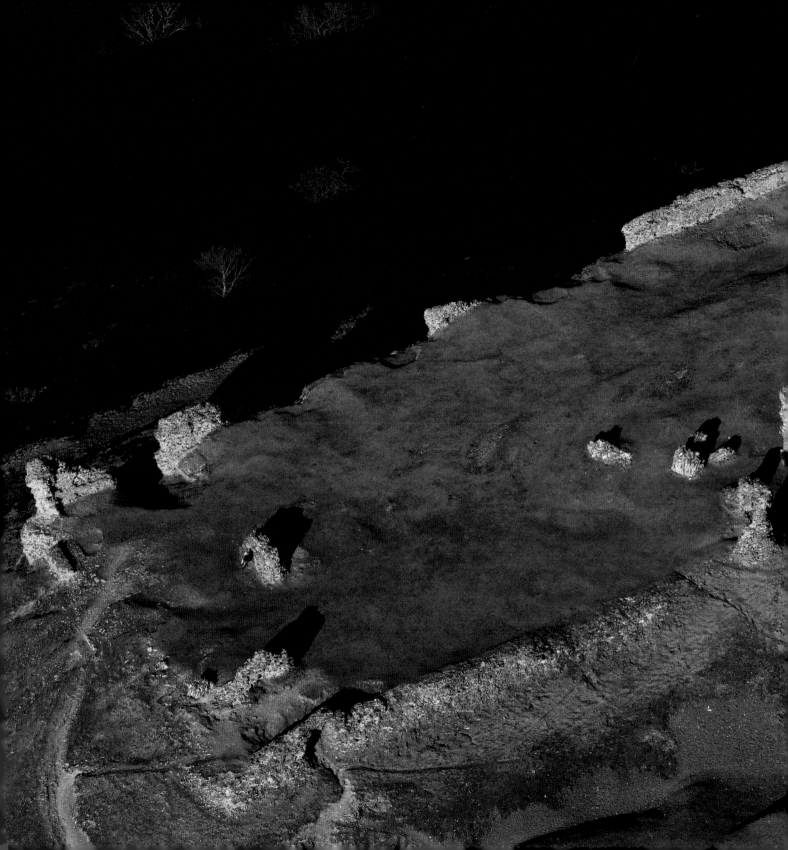

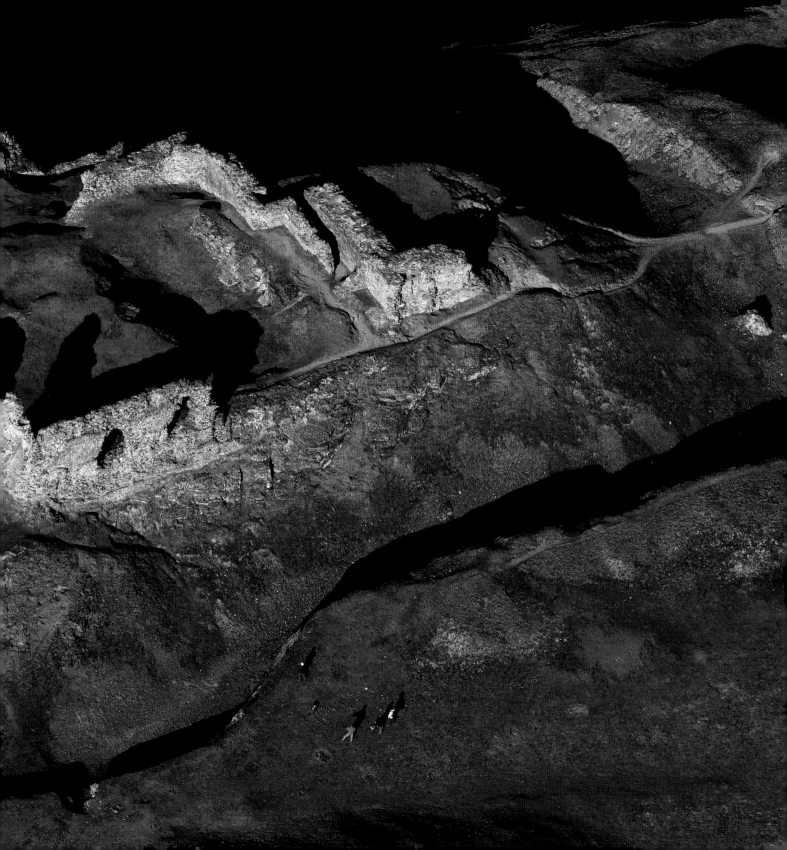

**Above:** The Pontcysyllte aqueduct, masterpiece of Thomas Telford and still the highest and longest aqueduct in Great Britain. Built from cast iron troughs on stone pillars, it was completed in 1805 and is now Grade I listed.

**Previous page:** Wrexham is the county town and commercial centre of North Wales. The town has grown since the Industrial Revolution arrived with the opening of an ironworks in 1762. In the centre stands the mediaeval St Giles's Church, built in 1506. Just left of the tower, behind the tree, is the grave of Elihu Yale, after whom Yale University in America was named.

**Overleaf:** Chirk Castle, built in 1295 for Edward I by Roger Mortimer. The castle was very badly damaged by cannon bombardment in 1659 during the English Civil War and was repaired afterwards, although the towers were rebuilt at a reduced height. The hedge line running from lower left, behind the castle, to mid right is Offa's Dyke.

**Above:** The Vale of Ffestiniog, with Maentwrog in the foreground and the River Dwyryd meandering up the valley. Up until 1868 the river was accompanied by the Cemlyn Canal, which was built to transport slate from the Diffwys Quarry. Maentwrog is largely an estate village, which was built with the profits from the slate industry for the employees of the Oakeley family from Tan y Bwlch, although its history goes back to the Roman river crossing. The wooded area on the slopes above the river includes a significant amount of ancient woodland, and parts of it are designated a 'Site of Special Scientific Interest'. If you look carefully you can just make out the Ffestiniog Railway winding its way from the lower left up to Dduallt Station by the small pool in the upper centre of the image.

**Left:** Llyn Trawsfynydd, the largest reservoir in Wales, was built as part of the Maentwrog hydro-electric power scheme in 1928 and is still in use today. It has outlived the nuclear power station at the top of the lake, which is now being decommissioned. Just on the right edge of the image is the Roman fort and amphitheatre at Tomen y Mur. In the foreground is the village of Trawsfynydd, and working its way up the right edge of the image you can still see the line of the old Great Western Railway, which connected Bala and Blaenau Ffestiniog.

**Above:** Llanrwst, with its 17th-century bridge, which was built to link the town with Gwydir Castle, nestles in the trees in the bottom-left corner. Running up the valley is the Conwy Valley Railway Line, which connects Blaenau Ffestiniog and Llandudno.

**Left:** Betws-y-Coed, showing the intersection of the River Llugwy and River Lledr. The town's name translates to in English as 'prayer house in the woods' and owes its origins to the 14th-century St Michael's Church, which is in the centre of the image between the station and the river.

**Previous Page:** Blaenau Ffestiniog is a town built on slate which was once shipped around the world. These days the world comes to Blaenau to marvel at the Llechwedd Quarry Museum and the Ffestiniog Railway.

**Overleaf:** The Conwy Valley with Llanrwst in the centre and the Great Orme in the background.

**Above:** Dolbadarn Castle was built by Llywelyn Fawr in the 13th century to protect the Snowdonia heartland. There may have been an earlier castle dating back to the Dark Ages, but the surviving architecture all dates from Llewelyn's time. The main tower was originally much higher and probably supported wooden hoarding, which was a fighting platform that encircled the top of the tower. In 1283 the castle was taken by the forces of Edward I and soon after was partly dismantled to provide building materials for Caernarfon Castle.

**Left:** Dinorwig Hydro-Electric Power Station, known as the Electric Mountain, was opened in 1984 and uses water from the Marchlyn Mawr reservoir on the summit. The water flows through a series of tunnels, deep within Elidi mountain, into a generator and then out into Llyn Peris at the bottom. It is then pumped back up during off-peak hours to help balance peak and off-peak electricity demand. The construction is on a massive scale, with 16km of tunnels, and required one million tons of concrete and 4,500 tons of steel to build.

**Above:** The National Slate Museum and the Llanberis Lake Railway. Originally built in 1870 as workshops for the quarry, the building now houses the museum and contains the largest working waterwheel in mainland Britain. The railway was originally built to transport slate to Port Dinorwig on the Menai Strait. The original railway closed in 1961, with the track being taken up, and the quarry closure followed in 1969. After the closure it was decided to convert it into a tourist railway, and after much rebuilding work through 1970 the little railway was opened.

**Right:** Llanberis on the shore of Llyn Padarn, with Anglesey and the Menai Strait in the background. The Llanberis Lake Railway tracks the right-hand edge of the lake with the end station in the town at the bottom of the image. Across the road is the terminus of the Snowdon Mountain Railway, another narrow gauge steam railway that takes visitors up a rack-and-pinion track to the summit of Snowdon.

**Above:** Walkers take a hard-earned rest at the summit of Snowdon, some 3,560 feet above sea level.

**Left:** Llechchog and Bwlch Main Ridge with Llyn Coch and Llyn Nadroedd below.

**Previous page:** The summit of Snowdon looking east, with the Clwydian Range in the background.

**Overleaf:** Snowdon, looking north towards the Great Orme, with the four-and-a-half-mile-long Snowdon Mountain Railway working its way up the mountain. Opened in 1896, the railway runs specially-built steam trains up the rack-and-pinion track with gradients of up to 1:5, and some of the original locomotives are still in service.

**Last page:** Snowdon looking north west to Llanberis and Llyn Padarn in the centre, with almost the whole of Anglesey visible in the background. Taken on an unusually clear day, Holyhead Mountain can just be seen on the horizon.